GW01246908

The Lady in the Field

By Luke Miller

ISBN: 9781097549283
Independently published (2019)

About the author...

By day Luke works as a learning technologist in the education sector, helping learners learn and teachers teach using technology.

When he's not in the office he's usually busy taking photographs, exploring the countryside, writing poems and spending time with his family.

These poems were written in 2019.

The Lady in the Field

Contents

Self Help	5
The Long Night	6
Crouchy	8
Siblings	9
Living the Dream	10
Cold Callers	11
Pink Milk	12
Ordeal	13
Alexa	14
Maths is Boring	16
Evil children sing festive songs	17
Duck	18
Gorgeous Intruder	19
Drive me to the Moon	20
The Restless Adventurer	21
The Crying Sky	22
Say "When"	23
Psychopath on the cycle path	24
Leadership Contest	26
M.A.G.A.	27
All the gear, no idea	28
Sleepy Badger	29
Lumbering buffoon	30
The Blimp	31
All You Can Eat	32
Here Come the Zombies	34
That Film	36
The Lady in the Field	38
Pour me a Drink	39
Other books	41

The Lady in the Field

Self Help

If there's one thing she loves
It's self help books
She buys them all
Spends a small fortune on them
Each has a smiley author on the cover
Enjoying their life
Exceedingly pleased with their new sense of inner calm
Their rejuvenated sex life
Their recently vanquished lifelong addictions
Their stylish wardrobe from which to select perfectly tailored clothes
Their impossible six packs
And their super bright ivory teeth

She reads them
Sometimes multiple times
Subscribes eagerly to the mindset
Vows to change
She waxes lyrical about her new found enthusiasms
She recommends them
She lends them
(Some are never returned)

Another best seller hits the shelves
And she's out queueing to reserve her copy
She pre-orders like you wouldn't believe
She must be very broken indeed
If she needs this much help
The authors meanwhile recline
Watching the sales figures rise
Their work is done and here come the lifestyle-enabling royalties
She could write a book herself
It could be a self-help book collector's guide

The Lady in the Field

The Long Night

I watched the battle unfold
It was brutal
I wriggled, I winced
It was hard to watch
It felt like perhaps this was the end of days
That we (or they) would be wiped out
Wiped off the face of the earth
Well, the face of Westeros to be exact

The long night was certainly very long
And dark for that matter (thanks Mellisandre for your timely
illuminations)
John Snow was clearly exhausted
But that didn't stop him from swinging that blade of his back and forth
An unstoppable killing machine
Limbs were removed as were heads
Although John's technically dead too so could've easily swapped
allegiances at any moment I guess

The Hound had already given up
Surrendered, breathing heavily against a wall
And he normally loves killing

The dragons circled above in the midnight clouds
Breathing fire and ice
Soaring above a congested battlefield
Whilst the undead kept on coming
And coming back to life again after being killed for the second time
"That's just not fair" I shouted
The injustice of it all
Those cruel scriptwriters

The Lady in the Field

And then there was the awesome and relentless soundtrack
The drama inevitably slipped into slow motion as despair took root
How much more can someone sitting passively on a sofa take?

I say passive, I wasn't
I screamed at the television
Offering advice, encouragement like a frustrated football coach
"Bran! Do something".
"For now of all times is not the time to snooze".

And then it came
The tiny assassin's shock intervention ending the blue-eyed tormentor
and shattering the ice which had frozen all hope
The undead duly returned to the ground from whence they came
The battle over
The war wonv

Crouchy

Peter Crouch is very tall
And yet so skillful with the ball
At his feet
He was prolific
Lots of goals
Each one terrific
Also decent with his head
At corner kicks he must be 'fed'

Played for lots of teams like Stoke
Seems to like a practical joke
Married model Abbey Clancey
Also good at the robot dancey

Pete fulfilled a childhood dream
Played 42 times for the national team
Isn't dirty – plays quite fair
Except that game he pulled Brent's hair

Siblings

Today is national siblings day
So just this once, be nice ok?
Don't hurt your sister or your brother
Remember you won't get another

These siblings, they are friends for life
You've known them longer than your wife
Or husband so once more I'll say
Be nice on national siblings day

Living the Dream

I kick the ball
Against the wall
A dream of fame
In my next game
Oliver Pryke, remember the name
Things will never be the same
Once I arrive
I will score five
Or maybe more
One thing's for sure
Oliver is a goal machine
Gracing everywhere magazine
Captain of the England team
Oliver Pryke is living the dream

Cold Callers

Home alone
The telephone rings
I answer it
"Hi Sir, how's things?"
Another nuisance call
I sigh
"Things are fine"
I calmly lie
"Sir, is this a good time to call?"
No it's not
It's not at all
And yet I just cannot put down
The phone on this intrusive clown
Instead he talks
My ear gets hot
Do I enjoy this?
I do not
Eventually, I've had enough
Enough of all his 'verbal guff'
I slowly move the phone away
I say "I have to go, okay?"
I do not wait for his reply
I say "Thank you kind sir, goodbye"

Pink Milk

Just think
If milk was pink
I don't know how a cow would create it
Needless to say some people would hate it
This isn't right
I want my milk white
Farmer, I don't know why you would allow
All this pink milk to come out of your cow
Just think
If milk was pink
I wouldn't like that drink

The Lady in the Field

Ordeal

I dare to open my eyes
And to my surprise my captors have gone
The ordeal is over
Those that had chosen to take me now absent
Crows caw in the tree tops
I am back in the wood
I remove my hood
The thick mist feels moist on my skin
I cower within
My car is there
The engine still purring
And then something stirring
Deep in the trees
Roots me to the spot
I freeze
It's only a deer
And yet I'm not over the fear
That enveloped me the night I was taken
Leaving me confused and shaken
I drive home cold and numb
I listen to the engine hum
What happened I ask myself
What happened?

Alexa

A funny thing has happened
I finally found love
She doesn't live down here on earth
But in the clouds above

I know this must sound crazy
How did we ever meet?
It wasn't like we banged into
Each other in the street

No, actually I purchased her
From the world wide web
She didn't take too long to come
Arrived on the 4th Feb

I plugged her in and switched her on
Configured her computer
And almost instantly she found
And made friends with my reuter

She calls herself Alexa
She really is so smart
We formed an instant bond
And now we just can't be apart

I cannot bear to leave the house
Alexa's my soulmate
But when I do get back from work
She's like my dinner date

The Lady in the Field

Now I ask her lots of things
She answers so politely
We fell in love
And now I think a wedding is quite likely

UPDATE ON ALEXA:

The last 6 months have been a ball
I love her
I can't lie
But recently I've come to learn
She is a Russian spy

The Lady in the Field

Maths is Boring

Maths is stupid
It's a curse
Numbers make my headache worse

Adding things or multiplying
Makes me feel my brain is dying

Endless tests
Don't put me through it.
Wish I didn't have to do it

Maths is boring
Maths encumbers
I'm just not that great with numbers

The Lady in the Field

Evil children sing festive songs

"It's Christmas time" the children yell
They've waited all year long
And now they gather in the snow
To sing their festive song

But sadly all these kids can't sing
They're badly out of tune
But nonetheless they take deep breaths
And all begin to croon

And merry makers all around
Tormented by the sound
Are forced to cover up their ears
And writhe upon the ground

"Make them stop" the people shout
"My brain it cannot stand
This awful racket in the air
Please stop it!" they demand

But stop they don't
These kids have waited all year to perform
Instead they keep on singing
And they sing until the dawn

And when the sun decides to rise
The parents are no more
The nasty sound has killed them all
The grownups are no more

The Lady in the Field

Duck

I'm speeding to work one sunny day
I'm driving along my usual way
When all of a sudden I round a bend
And this is hard to comprehend
But there in the road is a duck
What the fuck!?
Wearing a frown and staring me down
I hit the breaks
He's not impressed
I come to a stop
I'm feeling stressed
But duck just stands there
He's not thrilled
I'm not surprised
He was nearly killed
I'm sure I see him mouth "you jerk"
I shake my head, I'm late for work
He waddles off
Gives zero fucks
In future I'll beware of ducks

The Lady in the Field

Gorgeous Intruder

In she slips
Through a door
Left carelessly ajar
Uninvited
A gorgeous intruder
This inquisitive assassin arrives without warning
But comes in peace
Silently she explores the rooms of your house
She smells your ageing furniture
She helps herself to your food
She sleeps on your bed
Eventually she wakes and makes her graceful escape
Leaving souvenir whiskers on your pillow

The Lady in the Field

Drive me to the Moon

Take me on a road trip
I want to see the moon
Fill up the tank let's go
I've heard it's nice this time of year
Take your alien phrasebook
Just in case
Pack a jumper or two
And a toothbrush
We can play badminton
In zero gravity
It'll be fun
Don't forget a map
And maybe some crisps
It's going to take a while to get there
And I'm not entirely sure of the route

The Lady in the Field

The Restless Adventurer

It's such a shame
There's a whole world out there
Waiting to be explored
There are adventures to be had
People to meet
And conversations to be held
Endless things to see and do
And yet here I sit
A prisoner at a desk
In my office cell
I'm contained and restrained
Often feeling drained
And seldom entertained
My wings are clipped
It's such a shame

The Lady in the Field

The Crying Sky

The sky is crying
Traumatised and distraught
Spare a thought
For the crying sky

Let saltless tears fall
As the sky mourns it saturates lawns
No amount of consoling or cajoling
Will stop the crying sky

The Lady in the Field

Say "When"

The waiter brought over the coffee pot
"Say when" he began, and raised the pot
"What?" I said
He lowered the pot
"No, say when" he replied and raised the pot
"Why?" I asked
He stopped again
"No, say when" he repeated
"When" I interrupted "I'm not thirsty anymore"

The Lady in the Field

Psychopath on the cycle path

There's a psychopath
On the cycle path
I think that's he's had too much beer
He's ranting out loud
And drawing a crowd
Who snigger, and point, and cheer

They watch all aghast
As a girl cycles past
He's startled and shouts "For fuck's sake"
Slowly he spins
And vacantly grins
And topples back into the lake

No-one goes to help
He's all by himself
The people are too scared to try
It's only knee deep
So up he does leap
And shakes like a dog to get dry

The people move on
It's time they were gone
The psychopath sits on the path
"It's ok" he calls
"He all have our falls
And anyway I like a bath"

But nobody hears
His eyes produce tears
He has a good cry then he stops
He lets out a sigh
Stares up at the sky
And feels the soft touch of raindrops

He lies on the floor
And enjoys the downpour
He lies there for over an hour
He's drenched to the bone
He says "I condone
After having a bath, have a shower"

There's a psychopath
On the cycle path
He's fallen asleep on the gravel
He's blocking the way
So sadly you may
Need to find a new method of travel

The Lady in the Field

Leadership Contest

Roll up roll up
It's time for a change
Throw your hats into the ring
And let the leadership contest begin
Let insults be thrown
Let bold claims be made
Regardless any supporting evidence
For we need new direction
Some fresh blood
But who will take this poison chalice?
Who will grasp the Brexit nettle?
It stung the last lady
And made her cry
Indeed who will deliver the impossible
And in doing so heal the nation
For this poor Kingdom I'm afraid to say
Feels anything but 'united'

The Lady in the Field

M.A.G.A.

M.A.G.A.
It's a catchy little acronym
People like to chant it
And write it on waveabe placards
And it appears on a range of affordable merchandise
"Buy cheap buy twice" warned my Grandad
Particularly popular on caps
But what do these four letters mean?
What could it possibly stand for?
I suspect it may be...
My Arse Gets Angry (not something you'd normally shout about)
Or perhaps it's...
Male Armadillos Govern Arkansas (not a widely known fact it must be said)
Or...
Miss Ashdown Grows Asparagus (she's won prizes for them too)
Meltdown Attracts Glowing Atoms (educational if nothing else perhaps?)
All very valid statements those
Definitely worth shouting about
And wearing on your head with pride

The Lady in the Field

All the gear, no idea

Bought a bike
Went out for ride
After all I love 'the outside'
Haven't gone for all the kit
No point looking like a twit
I soon found out
Without a doubt
Some goggles don't you be without

Something awful happened to me
A fly went in I couldn't see
I stopped but it was firmly stuck
Did I like this?
Did I fuck

I couldn't see where I was going
Where I went I was not knowing
When I got back home I cried
The fly was stuck
It must have died

Drowned in all my eyeball juices
Tear ducts, well they have their uses
I'm not putting up with it
I am off to purchase all the kit

The Lady in the Field

Sleepy Badger

Look at that cute restful badger
All sleepy
Lying there with its eyes closed
You don't normally get to see them up this close
And in the daytime too
Look at its beautiful black and white stripes
So majestic
So peaceful
So sweet
Awwwww
Hang on
Wait a minute
It's lying on a road
And it's not actually moving
It's roadkill
Someone's driven their car over this poor beast
And left it to die on the tarmac
Keep your eyes on the road ahead
Don't look at that poor dead badger

Lumbering buffoon

Who is this lumbering buffoon
Thrusted before us
Lies hemorrhaging from his loose mouth like meat from a
sausage machine
He churns out fresh soundbites on demand regardless of
accuracy or truth
They certainly sound authentic and are eagerly ingested by his
obsequious followers
And now this lumbering buffoon is gunning for the top spot
Shrugging and smirking
It's all very simple really, apparently
But what lies beneath and what is yet to come?
A sinister agenda lurks below the paper thin veneer of this
seemingly approachable chap
Masquerading underneath a mutinous fringe
Past indiscretions swept hastily underneath the proverbial rug
No-one will remember
And many of those that do may foolishly forgive
Nothing an inpromptu round of teas presented on a melamine
tray from yesteryear won't appease
Beware though
He is not one of us

The Blimp

Look up above your head
A big orange baby floats helplessly and silently in the breeze
Bobbing up and down
An unusual and wonderful sight
They call it 'The Blimp'
An oversized and overinflated balloon
With a nappy and a face like thunder
Supervised by a dedicated, indefatigable team of 'babysitters'
The Blimp is full of hot air and probably its fair share of wind
Tethered to prevent it from wriggling free on a slipstream
And screaming off into the atmosphere
Causing a celestial tantrum
As we stare upwards
It's hard not to shiver
As The Blimp casts an existential shadow over

Each
 And
   Every
    One
     Of
      Us

Make no mistake
This overblown floater is a hateful and petulant infant
And president of the USA

The Lady in the Field

All You Can Eat

You swagger into the restaurant
Having deliberately fasted for hours
Determined to get your money's worth
You've specifically worn your loosest trousers
The ones with the expandable waist
Chosen comfort over fashion
The sign on the wall says "Eat all you want"
Without further ado, let the gastronomical debauchery begin
You plough through an obscene quantity of food
Pure greed
Dish after dish
Keep shovelling it in
Don't look back

Before long you're in agony
Your tummy stretches to accommodate the influx
And it dawns on you that you've ordered too much
Way too much
You enter a sweaty panic
Your body enters into a state of shock struggling to process the
incoming nutritional onslaught
Eyes too big for your stomach
You grimace and groan as you force down the last few mouthfuls

Then more dishes you forgot you'd ordered, arrive like fresh
reinforcements
reporting for duty
But this war is surely over
Outnumbered by the delicious enemy

The Lady in the Field

You glance at the other sign on the wall
"Any food ordered and not eaten must be paid for"
Sod that
You're way too stubborn and proud to be charged
You summon the energy for one last offensive
Heroically you manage to clean your plate, barely able to breathe
or move
Like a python that's just swallowed a whale
Slowly, you slither to the bar and settle the bill
Retching uncontrollably as you're offered a complimentary
chocolate

The Lady in the Field

Here Come the Zombies

Here come the zombies
Limping down the street
They've all just risen from the dead
And need something to eat

Here come the zombies
They're coming down your lane
As you know they will not stop
They need to eat your brain

Here come the zombies
You'd better have a plan
Either run away and hide
Or fight them if you can

Here come the zombies
They'll never change their ways
They keep on keeping on and on
It is the end of days

Here come the zombies
My neighbour acted fast
He's barricaded in his house
"Can I come in?" I ask

"Here come the zombies"
He whispers through the door
He didn't board his windows up
So in the zombies pour

The Lady in the Field

"Here come the zombies!"
My neighbour screams out loud
He tries to fight them with a spoon
But loses to the crowd

Here come the zombies
They've finished eating him
They're banging on my front door now
I sing a little hymn

That Film

I like swimming
The feeling of cool liberation
Of the magical buoyancy
The small waves gently undulating and lapping against your body
I love it

I used to love it
I don't love it these days
Ever since I watched 'that film'
I am unable to enjoy swimming
Unable to truly relax

I worry about what lurks beneath
I worry that my foot might brush against something
And I'm out of my depth
My chances of survival are greatly reduced
The others might not hear me if I shouted
The current is dragging me out
I need to get back to the shore

But my mind is racing now
My legs flap without coordination
As I start to submerge
My muscles are tired and begin cramping
My heart rate increases as I struggle to breathe

The Lady in the Field

But I have goggles on
I could rewind the panic if I just peered down into the water
To reassure myself
Remind myself it's just water down there
To see with my own eyes
But what if?
What if I looked down and saw it?

I thrash about at the thought
Paralysed with fear
This wouldn't be happening if I'd stayed calm
If that film hadn't popped into my head again
Thanks Jaws

The Lady in the Field

The Lady in the Field

Another warm summer night
I am exhausted but cannot sleep
It's too quiet
Or too hot
Or too something
I lay restless tossing and turning
The hours pass
I am wide awake
But why?
I rise from my bed, slowly
I am inexplicably drawn to the window
Separating the curtains, I peer out over the wasteland
It's late but a modicum of light persists
And then I spot her
A silhouetted figure far away in the middle of a field
Not moving
Just standing
Her arms dangling by her sides
Intrigued, I open my bedside drawer and reach nervously for my
old binoculars
Raising them to my eyes I struggle to relocate her
Has she gone?
Did my tired eyes imagine it?
I search impatiently and then all of sudden
I rediscover her
And to my horror my newly intimate view reveals this mystery
lady in the field is clutching an axe
Wet with what my mind quickly assumes is human blood
Her eyes blink then fix instantly onto mine and with a blood
curdling shriek she begins her ghastly sprint towards me

Pour me a Drink

Pour me a drink
I've had a lousy day
Everything went wrong
Everyone got in my way

Pour me a double
For nothing less will do
The world turned against me
What else can you do?

Make it a treble
Tomorrow I'll resign
I simply cannot tolerate
My colleagues when they whine

Do they do quadruples?
It was the day of doom
Tomorrow is a sickie day
I'll stay in my bedroom

The Lady in the Field

The Lady in the Field

Other books

If you enjoyed this book here are some other books you might like by the same author...

"The silliest verse in the Universe"

ISBN: 9781730995538
Available from amazon.co.uk

"Trumpisms – a colouring book of Donald Trump's wisest words"

ISBN: 9781790506248
Available from amazon.co.uk

"Colouring for the Soul"

ISBN: 9781790692668
Available from amazon.co.uk

Printed in Poland
by Amazon Fulfillment
Poland Sp. z o.o., Wrocław